T0024945

LeBron James
In His Own Words

LeBron James
In His Own Words

EDITED BY
**Elizabeth Pappas
and Emily Feng**

A B2 BOOK

AGATE

CHICAGO

Printed in the United States.

Library of Congress Cataloging-in-Publication Data

Names: Pappas, Elizabeth, editor. | Feng, Emily, editor.
Title: *LeBron James in his own words* / Edited by Elizabeth Pappas and Emily Feng.
Description: Chicago : Agate Publishing, Inc., [2023] | Series: In their own words
Identifiers: LCCN 2023032453 (print) | LCCN 2023032454 (ebook) | ISBN 9781572843288 (paperback) | ISBN 9781572848818 (epub)
Subjects: LCSH: James, LeBron. | African American basketball players--Biography. | Basketball players--United States--Biography. | Political activists--United States--Biography. | African American philanthropists--Biography.
Classification: LCC GV884.J36 L38 2023 (print) | LCC GV884.J36 (ebook) | DDC 796.323092 [B]--dc23/eng/20230719
LC record available at https://lccn.loc.gov/2023032453
LC ebook record available at https://lccn.loc.gov/2023032454

First printing: December 2023

10 9 8 7 6 5 4 3 2 1   23 24 25 26 27 28

B2 is an imprint of Agate Publishing. Agate books are available in bulk at discount prices. For more information, go to agatepublishing.com.

I think legacy will speak for itself. Who I am as a man and what I do off the floor defines my legacy more than what I do on the court.

—LEBRON JAMES

Contents

Introduction

Few people have been burdened with the expectations placed on a teenage LeBron James at the outset of his professional basketball career. Even fewer have exceeded them.

Drafted first overall at 18, he's since won four NBA championships, earned four MVP awards and two Olympic gold medals, and been selected for 19 All-Star teams. While he's become the all-time leading scorer in the NBA, he also ranks fourth in career assists, and he's famed for his devotion to team play.

But it's James's achievements off the court, from activism to business success, that truly set him apart as a cultural force. What it all comes back to, what's clearly his core motivation, is inspiring youth.

His own childhood was difficult. James's mother, Gloria, struggled to provide for him, and they moved from place to place in the seedier areas of Akron. James is devoted to his mother, who was loving and supportive even as she struggled to provide for her son on her own. When James was nine, his mother made a painful sacrifice, sending him to live with his football coach Frank Walker's family so that he could have a more stable home environment. James went from missing nearly as much school as he attended one year to winning the perfect attendance award the next.

The Walkers did more than help set James on the right path. They also handed him a basketball. Although he had started out playing football, James quickly became a basketball sensation. Not only was he breaking records left and right, by the end of his high school career, his games were selling out 9,000-seat arenas, with tickets reselling for $2,000. NBA scouts were calling him the "greatest player [they'd] ever seen." *Sports Illustrated* described him as "the Chosen One." Just before the NBA draft, he signed an $87 million deal with Nike; in fact, James had been on the Nike talent scouts' radar since he was in the eighth grade.

It was a lot to live up to. James started off strong. Right out of high school, his hometown Cleveland Cavaliers made him the first overall pick in the 2003 NBA draft. James was named Rookie of the Year, then was named an All-Star for the first time his second year. For those first two seasons, however, Cleveland missed the playoffs. Although James continued amassing personal success, he couldn't carry the Cavaliers to a championship during his initial stint with his hometown team.

Enter *The Decision*. In a 60-minute ESPN live special, James announced his move to the Miami Heat, where he formed a "super team" with fellow stars Dwyane Wade and Chris Bosh. The ill-considered special made James a villain to millions overnight. There was immense criticism about the spectacle; some felt it was narcissistic, while many more saw it as an affront to the Ohio fans who'd supported him since he was a teen. Some even burned his jerseys. However, James's remarkable ability to recover from missteps like *The Decision* is a key part of his greater significance.

During his four seasons in Miami, James eventually won two NBA championships and was twice named the NBA Finals MVP. His overt role in using his free agency to help form a team where he could have such success ushered in a new era of player empowerment; James helped shift the entire power dynamic between the league and its star players. James's appeal has been so great that he's even reshaped traditional fandom, with many now considering themselves "LeBron fans" instead of fans of any one team.

After finding success in Miami, James made the less controversial decision to return to Cleveland. Winning as many championships as he could for himself wasn't enough—he wanted to bring a title to his hometown, too. And he did: in his second season back, James led his team to a win that ended a 52-year championship drought.

After James moved once again to join the Los Angeles Lakers, he experienced the first significant injury of his career in his first season, missing the playoffs for the first time since 2005. The following year, in the 2019–2020 season, James was back, and the Lakers won James's fourth title from within the NBA's pandemic "bubble." Once again, James was named Finals MVP.

James has earned additional recognition for his success off the court. According to *Forbes*, James became a billionaire around 2022, the first active NBA player ever to do so (Michael Jordan hit the milestone after retirement). James is an astute businessman, owning SpringHill, a production company, and investing in numerous other enterprises. By relying not just on traditional endorsements but also partnerships and ownership/investments, James spearheaded a new form of sports marketing that afforded him another type of empowerment.

And James certainly makes that money work.

Success on the court isn't just about the game, or the money in his pocket. It's about showing kids what they can do. Beyond providing a living example and making substantial donations to various charities, James created his own charity, the LeBron James Family Foundation, to strengthen community and help families and children in Akron. Through the foundation, he created the I PROMISE School, providing education, food, and transportation to school for kids, and even GEDs and job help for parents, with a mission to support the most at-risk students.

James prioritizes inspiring his own children, too. He is clearly—and publicly—an involved father to his three children, cheering courtside at basketball games for his two sons and making cooking videos for YouTube with his daughter.

As a Black father specifically, James works to improve the future he'll leave to his children. James has always spoken up for what he believes in, including advocating for the Black Lives Matter movement. James launched More Than a Vote, a campaign to empower Black voters and combat voter suppression, during the NBA All-Star game in 2020, leveraging his visibility as an athlete to speak up for what's really important.

Part 1

EARLY LIFE

Childhood

MAN, I'M JUST a kid from Akron, Ohio. Wow, I'm truly blessed.

—**Twitter, December 22, 2011**

I WOULDN'T BE here today without my mom; she's like my best friend. Just knowing the sacrifices she, you know, had and did and everything was like for me. My mom was sixteen years old when she had me, and as a kid you don't really understand that. When you get older and you have kids of your own you're like, "Oh my god, you was a high school sophomore?!" Just knowing the commitment that she had for me and the sacrifice: there's nothing in this world I wouldn't do for her. I am who I am because of her.

—**NBA on TNT, February 19, 2023**

WHEN I WAS 5, some financial things happened, and I moved seven times in a year. We moved from apartment to apartment, sometimes living with friends. My mom would always say, "Don't get comfortable, because we may not be here long."

—ESPN, December 23, 2002

IN FOURTH GRADE, I missed 82 days of school. Out of 160.

—ESPN, December 23, 2002

I NEVER COMPLAINED. Never. We were already going through tough times. It doesn't make it any better if I'm complaining. My mother said it was time to go, I packed my little book bag and it was time to roll.

I remember my mother sitting me down and basically telling me because of certain situations, that she may be gone for a little while, that I was going to be living with one of my coaches. It was a challenge. That's all I cared about when I was growing up—if I was gonna be able to wake up and my mother was still alive or still by my side. That was—because I was already without a father, you know, and I didn't want to be without both of my parents so it was definitely scary and tough.

—*More Than a Game*, September 6, 2008

MY LIFE CHANGED. I had shelter and food.

—on moving in with coach Frankie Walker and family, ESPN, December 23, 2002

WHEN I WAS a kid, I wish I had the means and the ability to come up to Cleveland and just feel that energy and hopefully bump into one of those guys. Man, I had so many dreams of being an All-Star, when I was a kid growing up in Akron.

—2022 NBA All-Star Practice and Media Day press conference, February 19, 2022

[FIFTH GRADE] I played little league football for the first time, and in the six games I scored eighteen touchdowns and we won the city championship. And at that point I was like, "This is something I want to do." I loved the concept of [a] team.

—*Road Trippin'* podcast, March 2017

THE THING THAT I had on the court that I didn't have off the court was security. Because every day we went to the gym, I knew I was gonna get picked, we were gonna win basketball games or we were gonna win pickup games. I've always said it's home away from home for me.

—*More Than a Game*, September 6, 2008

I GREW UP in Akron, and there was no LeBron James to look up to.... You grow up in Chicago, you got Walter Payton, Michael Jordan. You grow up in Akron, you got Goodyear!

—*Esquire*, October 2008

I'M JUST A kid, I'm a kid from Akron, Ohio, that, statistically, I'm not even supposed to be here. ... The fact that I can walk into an NBA locker room, see "James" on the back of an NBA jersey; I'm already blessed. And then the man above gave me some athletic ability, gave me some talent, and I'm just trying to take full advantage of that.

—postgame interview, August 30, 2013

WHAT HELPED ME in school was sports. When I was 8, 9, that was the first time I started playing organized sports and I had coaches around me that stressed education and not being allowed to play if we weren't doing our schoolwork or being at school on time, things like that.

—ESPN, July 6, 2011

IT WAS TOUGH at times, but my mom, she kept it so real. . . . When I was growing up at times, on Father's Day, I would write my mother a card, wishing her Happy Father's Day. She was all I had.

—*Cleveland.com*, **June 19, 2016**

THEY SAID, "YOU are an inner-city kid, you are underprivileged, you live in poverty, you are not going to make it out." I mean, I would have lost a long time ago if I would have listened to what the narration of it all is.

—*Kneading Dough: The Podcast*, **March 5, 2019**

High School

HIGH SCHOOL FOR me is the best time of my life.

—*Road Trippin'* podcast, December 2017

IF YOU WERE an inner-city kid, you went to Buchtel. It was definitely an all-Black school so everybody expected us to be there.... Choosing to go to St. V was definitely bigger than just picking one high school over another. People look at you like you were choosing race.

—*More Than a Game*, September 6, 2008

I REALLY LIKE running on the football field.... It kind of takes me back to my high school days of playing the game of football. I just have a huge, deep love of the game of football.

—*The Tim Ferriss Show*, November 27, 2018

THAT 18-YEAR-OLD KID was just super excited to just start his journey, and I didn't know what to expect but I knew I belonged and I knew I could play in this league with the big boys.

—**ESPN, February 8, 2023**

GOING INTO SENIOR season, I started thinking "How am I gonna set our team up the right way to win it next year?" It was an eye-opener for me. On me being a leader that I wanted to be for our team.

—*More Than a Game*, **September 6, 2008**

WE WON BECAUSE we were together. We won because we respected Coach Dru as a coach, as a mentor, as a leader, and we had one goal and that was to win a national championship. And we wouldn't let nothing stand in our way.

—*More Than a Game*, **September 6, 2008**

EXTREMELY HAPPY FOR my guy [high school coach] Coach Dru!! You have played such a GIGANTIC part in my life growing up. Shaping me into the basketball player I've become but more importantly the man I've become! Thank you for EVERYTHING on and off the floor! You're the 🐐 !!! CONGRATULATIONS on the LeBron James arena court now being forever called "Coach Dru Joyce Court"! It's more than deserving and I appreciate you more than you'll ever know!! 🙏💜👑!!

—Facebook, July 24, 2022

SEEING WHAT WE had accomplished from a few months ago, being ranked 23rd, or years ago when we weren't ranked at all, or even more years ago when we weren't mentioned. The day it came out and we seen that St. Vincent–St. Mary was number one in the country, was probably one of the best days of our lives.

—*More Than a Game*, September 6, 2008

I go from $10 in my pocket to $100 million. In high school. Yup.

—*GQ*, February 18th, 2014

NINE YEARS IN the making. From fifth grade, we all dreamed about being able to play for the national championship. We had an opportunity in the eighth grade and failed. And now, a few years later, we have the same opportunity to do it.

—*More Than a Game*, September 6, 2008

MY GAMES GOT moved from our high school to the university, and our games started being televised. People would be out on the streets selling T-shirts with my likeness on it. I'm a pretty smart guy. And I wasn't getting none of it, and my mom wasn't getting none of it.

—*Shut Up and Dribble*, November 3, 2018

I WAS ON the cover of *Sports Illustrated* when I was in the eleventh grade, and I just thought I was doing another cover of another sports magazine. I didn't know how big it was at the time. I didn't know till I was like twenty-one years old how big *Sports Illustrated* was, and then I was like, Wow! I was pretty big in high school!

—*Esquire*, October 2008

MY WHOLE CAREER has been built off trial and error. I ain't have nobody when I came in at 18 [who] had an open-door policy for me, to help guide me through what I was about to go into. So it's been trial and error . . . just being a sponge.

—*Sports Illustrated*, August 30, 2022

PEOPLE ASK ME if it's a hard decision going to the NBA, but I've made harder decisions. Decisions about smoking or going to school, or stealing from a store or not stealing. Those are harder decisions.

—ESPN, December 23, 2002

BEING A FIRST-GENERATION money-maker in the household is a scary thing. For an 18-year-old, I go from sitting in classrooms in May . . . to being a multimillionaire a month later in June, which is insane. It's hard to kind of process that. It's a scary thing.

—*Kneading Dough: The Podcast*, **March 5, 2019**

AT EIGHTEEN YEARS old I knew I had to play the game, I knew I belonged in the NBA, but I didn't know what I could become at eighteen. I just knew that if I continue to put in the work and I continue to be true to the game then I could be one of the greatest players to ever play this game. I just always believed that.

—**postgame press conference, December 30, 2022**

Part 2

ON THE COURT

Cleveland Cavaliers

A year ago I was watching this at the start of the season. Now I'm finally here. It's a dream. This will never get old. When it does, that's when I'll stop playing.

—on playing his first NBA game, ESPN

I NEVER WANTED to leave Cleveland. My heart will always be around that area. But I also felt like this is the greatest challenge for me, is to move on.

—Modesto Bee, July 9, 2010

JUST TWO YEARS ago I decided to go back home. And my main goal was to bring a championship to a place that hadn't seen one in over 50-plus years. And to be able to bring it back to the hometown and do something that a lot of people didn't expect but we believed in, it meant everything.

—The Ellen Show, September 7, 2016

BY FAR THE best game I've been a part of.

—on game 6 of the 2013 finals, *Esquire*, October 2013

I'M GOING TO have to teach, lead, and inspire these guys. But my number one goal is to win a championship here. I think it would be the greatest achievement of my life as far as on the court.

—Akron Beacon-Journal, August 9, 2014

I WANTED TO have a great time, I wanted to dance—I couldn't. I just had nothing left in me. I gave everything I had to that game. I gave everything I had to that series, to that game.

—Road Trippin' podcast, December 2017

WHAT CAN I say CLEVELAND! Thank you! We did it for ya'll! #StriveForGreatness #TheLand #ChampionshipParade

—Instagram, June 22, 2016

This was bigger for me than the first and the second because of everything it represents.

—on winning his Cleveland championship,
Sports Illustrated, August 2016

LIFE. LIFE JUST changes. You have a mission
and you have more goals that you want to set out,
you know? When I won a championship here, I
didn't think that I would go anywhere, because I
felt like I was complete. And then I realized that
I still wanted to, I wanted to reach another level.
I wanted to reach another level, so it wasn't done.
My life goal wasn't complete.

—on what changed to make him leave Cleveland again,
The Athletic, February 19, 2022

Miami Heat

IN THIS FALL, this is very tough, in this fall I'm going to take my talents to South Beach and join the Miami Heat.

—*The Decision*, ESPN, July 8, 2010

I PLAY THE game fun, joyful. . . . That's what I lost last year. Going through my first seven years in the NBA I was always the "liked one" and to be on the other side—they call it the dark side or the villain or whatever they call it—it was definitely challenging for myself.

—on being viewed as the "villain" post–*The Decision*, ESPN, December 6, 2011

I STARTED TO learn, you can't really give a fuck about what people say no more. Everybody gonna critique everything that you do no matter what you do. That shit will creep into your mind, no matter if you believe it or not. . . . My first year in Miami I wanted to prove everybody wrong, and I literally lost myself in the moment . . . and afterwards we lost because I wasn't even there.

—*The Shop UNINTERRUPTED* podcast, March 2022

It basically turned me into somebody I wasn't. You start to hear "the villain," now you have to be the villain, you know, and I started to buy into it. I started to play the game . . . angry.

—ESPN, December 6, 2011

THE FRIENDSHIP WE'VE created our rookie year at pre draft camp was pure and that's why we stuck together from that point on! Obviously didn't know we would eventually become teammates and do the things we've done so far. I came to Miami for 2 reasons. To play with U and to win championships and I can't thank u enough for the sacrifice you've made since I arrived homie! No matter what happens in the future we stuck together like brothers for life.... Oh almost forgot u old as dirt! Boy you look 40. Hahaha!

—on **Dwyane Wade, Instagram, January 17, 2014**

WE KNOW WE'RE not going to be able to bury teams every day. . . . Will we win by 20 points-plus every game? No, but that's our mentality.

—*South Florida Sun-Sentinel*, **November 5, 2010**

THE BEST THING that happened to me last year was us losing the finals. And me playing the way I played, it was the best thing to ever happen to me in my career, because . . . I got back to the basics. It humbled me. I knew what it was going to have to take, and I was going to have to change as a basketball player and I was going to have to change as a person to get what I wanted.

—*Ottowa Citizen*, July 23, 2012

BEING A LEADER of my household, a leader of Miami, a leader of Team USA. It's the same exact thing. You can sense when a guy is frustrated— maybe doesn't feel involved enough in the offense. As leader you go over to him, you know, "How can I help?" Because at the end of the day, we all have one common goal—and that's to be great.

—*GQ*, February 18th, 2014

THAT'S AN ICONIC photo in sports. Forever . . . when he dropped it off to me he already knew what was going to happen before it happened. It was just like, "We here. And we're here to do something special."

—on the iconic sports photo featuring Heat teammate Wade spreading his arms in celebration as Lebron dunks mid-air in the background, **ESPN**

FROM THE TIME me and D-Wade got together, I just told him: "Just throw it anywhere, I'll go get it. Anywhere you throw it, I'll go get it." And that's what it was.

—on James and Wade playing together, **ESPN**

THE CHAMPIONSHIP LASTS (he snaps his fingers) just like that. The confetti rains, you go into the locker room, pop the champagne, you do the media, you have the parade, and then it's over. It's over.

—*Honolulu Star-Advertiser*, October 29, 2013

Los Angeles

Lakers

MY DECISION WAS based solely on my family and the Lakers.

—*New York Times*, **October 18, 2018**

THIS IS A historic franchise and, to be a part of this, is something that I'll be able to talk about, and my grandkids and kids will be able to talk about that their "paw paw" or their "dad" played for the Los Angeles Lakers.

—**postgame press conference, October 11, 2020**

IT'S PRETTY AMAZING. That's pretty much how I'mma be when I'm done playing. Being able to come back and watch this beautiful game.... We all root for one another no matter past, present, or future.

—**on Kobe watching his game, postgame locker room interview, January 26, 2020**

We play games without the fans? Nah, that's impossible. . . . I ain't playing if you don't have the fans in the crowd. That's who I play for.

—*New York Times,* March 9, 2020

I THINK PERSONALLY thinking I have something to prove fuels me. . . . It fueled me over this last year-and-a-half since the injury. It fueled me because no matter what I've done in my career to this point, there's still rumblings of doubt.

—*Sports Illustrated,* October 26, 2020

IT'S MY RESPONSIBILITY to put this team in a position to be successful. . . . They look at me as a leader. And it's my job, not only on the floor to get guys opportunities, get them great looks, but to inspire them, as well. To show them that I'm not slowing down, even at this stage of my career.

—*New York Times,* March 9, 2020

WE WERE ALL excited to get back, we were excited to play basketball again. I mean, we stopped playing in March. So we were all excited. But you don't really know what you are getting yourself into until you get inside the bubble and they tell you, "That right there, you cannot go outside that gate."

—*Road Trippin'* **podcast, December 2020**

IT MEANS SOMETHING. Something more than just a uniform. It represents an individual who gave the franchise 20 years of his blood, sweat, and tears and his dedication to his craft, both on and off the floor, to make that franchise be proud of him, and hopefully vice versa.

—on "Black Mamba" alternative uniforms post–Kobe Bryant's death, ESPN, October 7, 2020

YOU PLAY THE game the right way, and I think the basketball gods kind of give back to you.... We play hard. We fight. We scrap, and then live with the results and go from there. So we've given ourselves a good chance just to be the best team we can be.

—*The Athletic*, **January 8, 2023**

THIS WAS AN unbelivable achievement for our franchise, an unbelivable achievement for myself, what I was able to do for this team and what this team was able to do for me. And I want more. I'm not settled, and I'm not satisfied.

—**on winning the 2020 NBA championship,** *Road Trippin'* **podcast, December 2020**

WE'RE CHAMPIONS!!!!!!!!! IT just now hit me!! #LakerNation 🖤🤍🏆

—**Twitter, October 12, 2020**

WHEN I PLAYED for Miami, I rooted for the
Marlins and I rooted for the Dolphins. Not saying
they were my favorite teams, but at the end of the
day I root for them and I want them to be as great
as they can be. When I was in Cleveland, I rooted
for the Browns. . . . We root for our respective
clubs, because when we win, and we all win, it
brings so much more joy to our communities,
just a positive influence. Now that I'm here
playing for the Lakers, besides the Clippers, I
root for everybody.

—*Road Trippin'* podcast, December 2020

IT DOESN'T MATTER where it happens if you win
a championship. . . . A bubble, Miami, Golden
State—it doesn't matter. When you get to this
point, it's one of the greatest feelings in the world
for a basketball player to be able to win at the
highest level.

—*New York Times*, October 11, 2020

WE NEED SOME really nice things/ We need some really big RINGS/ I got a really big team/ Better be comin' with no strings! Man WHAT A TIME!🔥

—**Facebook, December 23, 2020**

Achievements

I GAVE EVERYTHING that I had. I pour my heart, my blood, my sweat, my tears into this game. And, against all odds, I don't know why we want to take the hardest road, I don't know why the man above give me the hardest role, but the man above don't put you in situations that you can't handle.

—on coming back from a three-game deficit in the 2016 finals, postgame interview, December 24, 2016

IT'S SOMETHING I never set out to do. I'm not even a score-first guy when it comes to playing basketball. I love getting my teammates involved and seeing my teammates be excited about scoring and me getting assists.

—on reaching 30,000 career points, NBA.com, January 23, 2018

You guys
don't know
me by now?
I don't play
for individual
stats. I play
to win.

—*Miami Herald*, February 13, 2011

WHEN IT COMES to the record, I felt pretty good, I felt in a good rhythm and once I get in a good rhythm I feel like I make any shot on the floor. . . . I was able to get it and it touched nothing but the bottom of the net and that was pretty cool.

—on becoming the leading scorer in NBA history, ESPN, February 8, 2023

I WANTED TO be the Rookie of the Year my rookie year, I wanted to be an All-Star, I wanted to win championships, I wanted to be the MVP of the league, I wanted to be Defensive Player of the Year. . . . I never, ever was like, "I wanna break the all-time scoring record." It's never ever been a thought of mine and the fact that I'm like literally right here, it's mind-blowing.

—ABC News, February 8, 2023

NOT AT ALL. I didn't get to this point in my career by thinking about records or how many points I have. . . . Maybe when I get super-duper close, maybe it will be at the back of my mind or the front of my mind. But I never put that type of pressure on myself. I just go and play.

> —when asked if he thought about breaking Kareem Abdul-Jabbar's career scoring record, *New York Times*, February 1, 2023

I DON'T LIKE being singled out as a scorer. I've always prided myself in being a pass-first guy—a guy who can make everybody feel comfortable.

> —on being labeled a 'scorer' about 10 days from breaking NBA all-time scoring record, ESPN, February 7, 2023

I SEE IT and I smirk. When they talk about the best scorers who ever played the game, my name never comes up. They have no choice now.

> —on breaking the NBA all-time scoring record, ESPN, February 7, 2023

I'VE NEVER GONE into the season saying, "OK, league MVP is what I want to be." I've gone into the season saying, "OK, I want to be the MVP of this team; I want to be the best player in the world," and how I approach my game every day, how I take care of my body every day has resulted in that [award].

—ESPN, March 5, 2020

LAST WEEK MESSED around and got a triple..... I mean a Scoring Record! Man what!!! This is still not hitting me yet. So surreal!! Wow wow wow man!! To all my fans who captured that moment there inside Crypto Arena that night (YOU'RE AMAZING & THANK YOU) and to all my fans all over the United States and The World (YOU'RE AMAZING & THANK YOU).

—Instagram, February 14, 2023

That's why I started [the media company] Uninterrupted. I got sick and tired of media changing the narrative or picking their own narrative about what I was doing.

—*Sports Illustrated*, August 30, 2022

The Game

I IMPROVED OVER the course of my career. So, there's never been a ceiling too high or I've never put a ceiling on what I can accomplish.

—**ESPN, November 3, 2017**

I COULD DO all the training, I could do all the ice bags, the NormaTec, and everything that we do that we have as far as our recovery package while I'm up, but when you're getting that good sleep, you just wake up and you feel fresh. You don't need an alarm clock. You just feel like, okay, I can tackle this day at the highest level that you can get to.

—*The Tim Ferriss Show*, **November 27, 2018**

IT COMES BACK to that patience, of learning [the players'] mindsets, learning how can you get the most out of them, what triggers them to be their best, what triggers them to not be their best. You learn that over time.

—*The Tim Ferriss Show*, **November 27, 2018**

Leadership is not a one-day thing. . . . Leadership is consistent. And I believe having longevity in the space I'm in is also consistency as well, not only on the floor but off the floor as well.

—*The Tim Ferriss Show*, November 27, 2018

IF YOU CHALLENGE me to score, I'm going to score. And at the same time I'm going to keep my guys involved. I play for the team.

—*Road Trippin'* **podcast, December 2020**

THE ONLY THING that bothers me is when I'm not able to play because of an injury. That bothers me when I'm not able to be on the floor. Because I never know if it was that game or that city that a kid was coming to come see me and I'm not playing in that game. That's the only thing that kinda bothers me.

—*The Shop UNINTERRUPTED* **podcast, March 2022**

I GIVE EVERYTHING to the game and I hope it continues to give back to me!

—**Twitter, January 17, 2013**

Every day is a dream. I'm so blessed that this game of basketball has taken this kid from Akron around the globe. I never take a single moment for granted.

—Instagram, September 14, 2016

I'M OBSESSED WITH it. Win or bust. What makes me have sleepless nights is when you don't have everyone that feels the same way on your club.

—*The Shop UNINTERRUPTED* podcast, July 2022

I AM ADDICTED to the process. I'm addicted to the process.

—*Road Trippin'* podcast, March 2017

I'VE ALWAYS LOVE[D] seeing the success of my teammates!! Seeing my teammates score always meant more to me than me scoring! I can't do anything without those guys every single night. Their hardwork, dedication, professionalism, etc, etc has put me in the position I am today.

—Instagram, February 24, 2015

WHO KNEW A three-year-old boy's dream and a Little Tikes hoop could lead to all this?

—Instagram, April 3, 2016

MY LOVE FOR this game is insane and drive[s]
me crazy! Which I LOVE!! Nothing to me is
better than the process of feeling uncomfortable
as u try and push to improve on your skill/talent.
I have no ceiling and I refuse to fall into the trap
of complacency!

—**Instagram, August 23, 2017**

A LOT OF players know how to play the game,
but they really don't know how to play the game,
if you know what I mean. They can put the ball
in the hoop, but I see things before they even
happen. You know how a guy can make his team
so much better? That's one thing I learned from
watching Jordan.

—*Sports Illustrated,* **February 18, 2002**

I TRAVEL ALONG this journey in my own lane/ I only compete with myself. I am my own biggest critic and fan at the same damn time frame! Catch me if you can! 🙏🏿🤎👑 #ThekidfromAKRON 🐐 #KingMe👑

—**Facebook, January 10, 2021**

TO FEEL THAT adversity, to feel that tension is what brings out the best in us, you know. Your whole motivation besides trying to win the game, obviously, is shutting up the opposing fans and opposing crowd and making them go home and get no sleep because of you.

—*Jimmy Kimmel Live,* **July 14, 2021**

I JUST FEEL so good about the game. I feel like I owe it to the game, as long as I could go out and still play at a high level, I feel like it's important for me to continue to inspire the youth, continue to inspire my teammates, try to inspire myself. And I still have championship aspiration.

—**ESPN, February 7, 2023**

SOMETIMES I WAKE up and I'm like, "Oh, I ain't gonna make it tonight, I just feel it. These twenty years have got to me tonight. It ain't gonna be good tonight." And then I get out on the floor and I'm running past, you know, twenty-one-year-olds, jumping higher than twenty-three-year-olds, and I feel real good on how I'm playing the game, not only physically but more importantly just, like, mentally.

—**ESPN, February 7, 2023**

CHEMISTRY IS ALWAYS very key. . . . In my experience I've been able to be a part of both where you have some inexperienced lineups or inexperienced teams. . . . And then, obviously, I've been a part of teams that have been through so many battles that adversity meant nothing, you know, because that's when you literally, like, thrive [is] in those moments, those adverse moments.

—**postgame press conference, December 17, 2022**

I'VE ALWAYS LOVED the excitement that I gave my teammates by giving them the ball, seeing them score since I first ever started playing the game of basketball. That's always been, like, the greatest thing on the floor for me.

—**postgame interview, January 26, 2020**

I KNOW WE win. But I don't really know what happened.

—**on watching tape,** *Sports Illustrated,* **August 2, 2016**

TO BE ABLE to play at this level, you know, twenty years in, and the minutes I've played, the games I've played . . . to still be at the apex of my game, it's a pretty surreal feeling. So, you know, hopefully I can continue it, but at the end of the day it's just been a pleasure to be in this league for twenty years. . . . I've had a hell of a ride.

—*House of Highlights,* **February 8, 2023**

I'm a team-first guy when it comes to understanding that you can't be great in this league without great teammates, great coaches, that prepare [you] every single day to be great.

—ESPN, February 8, 2023

Part 3

OFF THE COURT

Philanthropy

I KNOW A lot comes with being a professional athlete. That's also being a role model to a lot of kids that look up to me. This automatically comes with it. And I have nothing but time for kids. I could easily be at home and just relaxing. . . . But the opportunity to be here and giving back to these kids, I'm happy to do it.

—on donating to the Boys & Girls Clubs of America and spending time with the children who benefited through the donation, ESPN, March 2, 2011

HUMBLED & UNBELIEVABLY proud to announce the #LJFF I PROMISE Institute at @UAkron!! Go back. Invest. Rebuild. Change. That's our duty.

—Twitter, October 12, 2016

To be an African American kid and grow up in the inner city with a single-parent mother and not being financially stable and to make it to where I've made it today, I think I've defeated the odds, and I want every kid to know that and everybody to know that the youth, they can do it as well.

—ESPN, February 18, 2018

Tomorrow is going to be one of the greatest moments (if not the greatest) of my life when we open the #IPROMISE School. This skinny kid from Akron who missed 83 days of school in the 4th grade had big dreams...big dreams for the kids in Akron to give them everything they could need to find their passion, give back to our community, and change the world!! This school is that. The people are that. Akron is that.

—Twitter, July 29, 2018

IT MEANS EVERYTHING to not only myself, not only to my foundation, but to my hometown. And those 240 kids that's in there right now, I walked the same streets as those kids, I had the same dreams, the same nightmares, the same upbringing as those kids, so I know everything that they're going through. And for me to be able to have a thought about having an at-risk school and then have it come to fruition and us opening a month ago. . . . By 2021, we'll have grades first through eighth, over 1,200 kids. It's a dream come true for me and I hope that the dream coming true for me will make their dreams become a reality. It's unbelievable.

—The Ellen Show, September 12, 2018

So WE'VE GIVEN the opportunity for parents in these households that didn't graduate high school to get an opportunity to graduate, get a GED as well so they can feel like, parents do their work, kids do their work, they feel like, listen, we all empowered.

—The Daily Show, August 17, 2016

I had the vision of wanting to give back to my community. The people around every day are helping that vision come to life. . . . Half the battle is trying to engage them and show that there's always going to be somebody looking out for them.

—*New York Times,* April 12, 2019

YOU KNOW, FOR me, personally, I know where
I come from, growing up in inner city in Akron,
Ohio. And I know the challenges that kids
have. And for our society to become as great as
it should be, I think it starts from the ground
up. And it starts in our communities, our own
communities, going back into our communities,
using our resources, using our knowledge.
Anybody can lend money or anybody can go give
an appearance, but I think actually being there
and them seeing you gives them—it gives the kids
hope. And without the kids we have no future.

—*The Daily Show,* August 17, 2016

CHANGE DOESN'T HAPPEN with just talk! It
happens with action and needs to happen
NOW! For my @IPROMISESchool kids,
kids and communities across the country,
it's on US to make a difference. Together. ✊🏿
#BlackLivesMatter

—Twitter, August 27, 2020

THESE KIDS ARE doing an unbelievable job, better than we all expected. . . . When we first started, people knew I was opening a school for kids. Now people are going to really understand the lack of education they had before they came to our school. People are going to finally understand what goes on behind our doors.

—*New York Times,* April 12, 2019

WHEN WE STARTED this work in education with my foundation, we never dreamed we'd be owning buildings and developing new properties. . . . As we dug deeper into the work, we learned what it takes to create real, visible change. And that's listening to what our community needs and then rolling up our sleeves and getting to work.

—*New York Times,* March 10, 2021

I believe in order for us to ultimately be as great as we can be as a nation that all of us have to go back into our communities and lend our hand. It starts brick by brick. It starts person by person. Family by family. Kid by kid.

—on the LeBron James Family Foundation, ESPN, August 17, 2016

IT MEANS SO much because, as a kid growing up in the inner city and a lot of African American kids, you don't really think past high school. . . . You hear high school all the time, and you graduate high school, and then you never think past that because either it's not possible or your family's not financially stable to even be able to support a kid going to college.

—on his 4-year college scholarship for I PROMISE kids,
ESPN, August 14, 2015

ANYTIME YOU CAN go back into your community, or even if it's not your community, give back to kids. . . . They feel like nobody cares about them, and there is so much talent. Not only in the inner city, but that's what I know, that's where I'm from.

—*Road Trippin'* podcast, February 2018

IF IT'S SOMETHING they have passion about we try to bring it to the school and try to give them the resources to see if we can tap into it.

—*SmartLess* podcast, July 2021

Humbled & proud to announce the establishment of the LeBron James Family Foundation I PROMISE Institute at The University of Akron. Scholarships weren't enough. We're investing our time, talent, and resources every day with our team, partners, and UA to give my kids every opportunity possible for them to be successful. I won't be satisfied with them just getting to college or tech school. We need them to graduate. This is our home. This is my home.

—Instagram, October 12, 2016

This!!! This is what all the blood, sweat, and tears have led to. 🙏 We've been hard at work to change the lives of kids & families in Akron. It takes time. It takes the right team... but this is what redefining community looks like. 🖤🖤 This is our next chapter for the LeBron James Family Foundation 🚀

—on the LeBron James Family Foundation's efforts to support education, Facebook, December 15, 2020

Advocacy and Activism

GROWING UP IN the inner city, seeing how underprivileged Black people are, I always felt like if I had an opportunity to be able to have any type of platform I always wanted to give back to that, I always wanted to be able to use my voice, and the people that grow up like me to be able to understand that we do have power, we do have an opportunity to make people understand that there is good in love.

—postgame press conference, January 17, 2023

BASKETBALL IS OUR vehicle but equality is our mission – stand for something positive and do what you can to make a difference!!

—Instagram, February 26, 2018

WHEN GEORGE FLOYD was murdered and all of us organized in the streets and on social media to demand action, More Than a Vote came together. We are a coalition of Black athletes using our influence to educate, energize and protect Black voters.

—**Instagram, August 17, 2020**

WE ALL HAVE moments in our lives where we know who we are and we know what we're about. And it's about growth. I've grown over the course of my career. I've grown over the course of being an 18-year-old kid that came into the league in 2003, to a 35-year-old man that's a husband and a father of three kids. I've grown to know who I am and what I stand for. And it's not just about me, it's about my people. That's why I'm leading the charge.

—**on his More Than a Vote initiative,** *New York Times,*
October 21, 2020

EVERYONE IN CALIFORNIA: call your politicians and tell them to support SB 206! This law is a GAME CHANGER. College athletes can responsibly get paid for what they do and the billions they create.

—**Twitter, September 5, 2019**

ONE OF MY first goals is to continue to inspire the youth to want to play this game of basketball or be better in whatever that they do. . . . Inspire millions no matter what they've gone through in their lives at that point in time, they can always overcome it.

—**postgame press conference, June 21, 2013**

IT WASN'T EVEN like Barack and Michelle was going into the White House. It was like every African American in America is going into the White House.

—***Shut Up and Dribble,* November 17, 2018**

I know my purpose and it's for damn sure bigger than just dribbling a basketball.

—Instagram, February 17, 2018

THE NUMBER ONE person in America [President Trump] is someone who doesn't understand the people. And really don't give a fuck about the people.

—Shut Up and Dribble, **November 3, 2018**

WITHOUT THOSE GUYS [athletes such as Bill Russell, Kareem Abdul-Jabbar, and Oscar Robertson] standing for something that was more than dribbling a basketball . . . I'm not sitting here talking to you.

—Shut Up and Dribble, **November 3, 2018**

IT MEANS SOMETHING . . . something more than just a uniform.

—on wearing warm-up shirts that read "VOTE,"
***New York Times,* October 11, 2020**

YES, WE WANT you to go out and vote, but we're also going to give you the tutorial. . . . We're going to give you the background of how to vote and what they're trying to do, the other side, to stop you from voting.

—*New York Times,* July 30, 2020

WHEN YOU WAKE up and you're Black, that is what it is. . . . It shouldn't be a movement. It should be a lifestyle. This is who we are. And we understand that. And we know that for one step that someone else might have to take, or for one yard someone else may have to take, we know we've got to take five more steps. . . . I don't like the word "movement" because, unfortunately, in America and in society, there ain't been no damn movement for us.

—*New York Times,* July 24, 2020

IT WAS A message to the family. That I'm sorry for their loss, sorry to his wife. That's what it's about. I think everybody else gets caught up in everything else besides who's really feeling it, and that's the family. That's what it's about.

—on wearing an "I Can't Breathe" shirt after the killing of Eric Garner, ESPN, December 8, 2014

THERE'S NO ROOM for guns, first of all, but then for violence towards kids or anybody. But, having kids of your own, I see the news go across my phone and I'm sitting there in front of my three kids, so it automatically just hit me.

—ESPN, October 2, 2015

THAT'S HOW AMERICA has been for a long time and the shit ain't going to change, but what will change is how guys in power [respond]. And what will change for me, and what has already changed, is I will continue to speak up for my people no matter if [society] likes it or not.

—ESPN, February 25, 2022

You're not a criminal because you put a hood over the top of your head. It's a uniform for us. That's what we do. That's what we wear. We don't have the luxury of wearing suits or having button-downs. We don't have the means to get sweaters and things of that nature. Our uniform is T-shirts, hoodies, and shorts. That's our uniform growing up as Black kids in the inner city.

—on the killing of Trayvon Martin, ESPN, February 25, 2022

I'm a Black man with a bunch of money and a crib in Brentwood, and having the word "n-----" spray painted over my gate, that lets you know I still have a lot of work to do. . . . No matter how far you come, there are always people who want to let you know that you are still beneath them.

—ESPN, February 15, 2018

No matter how much money you have, no matter how famous you are, no matter how many people admire you, being Black in America is tough. And we've got a long way to go for us as a society, and for us as African Americans, until we feel equal in America.

—pre-game press conference, June 1, 2017

HATE, IN AMERICA, especially for an African American, is living every day. Even though it's concealed most of the time—people will hide their faces and will say things about you and then when they see you they smile in your face— it's alive every single day. And I think back to Emmett Till's mom, actually. It's kind of one of the first things I thought of. And the reason that she had an open casket is because she wanted to show the world what her son went through as far as the hate crime, and being Black in America.

When you're born African American, you always got to do things more than the norm just because you're Black. . . . We understand that we have to work even extra hard because there's just always a "prove" thing. We always got to try to prove ourselves.

—ESPN, November 19, 2017

I'VE ADMIRED LEADERS like MLK, he is one of the greatest leaders that I've had the opportunity to read about and watch from afar, obviously; Muhammad Ali, as well, is one; Barack Obama is another, and then my mother. I believe my mother is one of the greatest leaders just in the fact of being a single parent mother in the inner-city without any financial stability and being able to raise a kid on her own at age sixteen.

—*The Tim Ferriss Show,* November 27, 2018

AS THE PLAYERS, to be able to use the NBA platform and us be able to go out there and speak about systemic racism, police brutality, voter suppression, everything that was going on, gave us an opportunity. . . . Strength in numbers. We actually saw that in the bubble.

—*Road Trippin'* podcast, December 2020

YOU WANT TO see all this change, but I felt like those conversations and that change needed to happen before we stepped back on the floor. And we had a conversation where two or three guys from each respective team, the coaches, and we had a huge Zoom call with the owners, all thirty owners. To talk about some of the changes, or some of the things that we can do to help create change while we're still playing the game. Because a lot of people was saying, "Well, once you guys get to playing basketball, you guys are going to forget about us." And I didn't want that to happen. . . . I wanted to see real change.

—*Road Trippin'* podcast, December 2020

ANY ONE OF us in this world, or in America, where we live in, if you do something that harms other people, you are held accountable. And we felt like at that point in time, the police were not being held accountable.

—*Road Trippin'* podcast, December 2020

I WANT EVERY kid, no matter their ability, gender, race, to #seethepossible around them and #striveforgreatness.

—Twitter, April 3, 2017

WE'RE TRYING TO figure out ways right now we can continue to implement change in the communities, not only in my home community of Akron, Ohio, but communities all over America and hopefully create change in the world, as well.

—*Road Trippin'* podcast, December 2020

ONE OF MY biggest goals was like, how . . . can I create voice and power for us: as Black creators, as Black people?

—*The Shop UNINTERRUPTED* podcast, October 2022

MY WHOLE MISSION in life is to speak for my people.

—*The Shop UNINTERRUPTED* podcast, June 2022

At the end of the day, it's very rare that you can play professional sports but be known for something bigger than that when you're done. It's very rare.

—*Road Trippin'* podcast, December 2017

THE MOST DISRESPECTED person on earth is THE BLACK WOMAN! I promise you I'll do my best to change this as much as I can and even more!! LOVE to you QUEENS all over this country and beyond!

—Twitter, September 23, 2020

TO MY BROTHERS and sisters in sports and arts. We have incredible influence in our community. We need to use this moment to demand change. I gotta be honest...I struggle with what to demand because so damn much needs to change.

—Instagram, June 23, 2020

BLACK VOTERS CAME through...again. Be proud as hell but do not stop! We must stay organized and keep working. We just tipping off.

—Instagram, November 6, 2020

THERE IS NO place for misogyny, sexism, and racism in any work place. Don't matter if you own the team or play for the team. We hold our league up as an example of our values and this aint it.

—on misogyny and racism from then-owner of the Phoenix Suns Robert Sarver, Facebook, September 14, 2022

Family

IN ORDER FOR me to be able to accomplish what I've done over these two decades, I had to have the rock and the support that I got from Savannah. There's no way that I would've been able to enjoy these moments or to be able to commit to my craft—she's allowed me to do this.

—**NBA on TNT, February 19, 2023**

I TRY TO set an example of how I treat their mother on a day-to-day basis, how I treat their grandmothers, you know, how I treat their little sister. How I treat others with kind[ness] and patience, so hopefully I can instill life skills in them, so when they walk out in the real world they'll be able to behave themselves like men.

—**ESPN, February 8, 2023**

I WANTED TO be a part of the statistics that breaks the mode of fathers running out on their kids. That was something that I obviously went through and I knew from Day 1 that wasn't going to be me.

—*Cleveland.com,* **June 19, 2016**

HERE'S TO ALL the fathers that didn't have the blueprint but figured it out along the way!! 🖤🙏👑

—**Twitter, December 12, 2022**

MY MOTHER BROUGHT me up real good. She taught me so [many] things . . . besides basketball, and I just hope that helps me be level-headed.

—*Shut Up and Dribble,* **November 3, 2018**
[footage from 2001]

WHEN U HAVE someone that's always there for you no matter the ups and downs in life, it makes it all worth living for!

—**Instagram, September 18, 2013**

YOU CAN'T HAVE any expectations just because you're . . . LeBron's son. You have to be even more cautious, because you just don't know. And that is a scary thing, being a Black father with a kid that drives. . . . These kids are so well known, and they're leaving the house, and [our] daughter's in school.

—***Sports Illustrated*, August 30, 2022**

WE ALL SUPPORT each other. We want each other to be great. My job is to send it back to him [Bronny] and him to send it to his little brother, little brother to his little sister.

—***Sports Illustrated*, August 30, 2022**

Basketball has given me a lot, has taken me all over the world, has inspired a lot of people, but you know, for me, being a father is even more dynamic, way more driven than the game.

—ESPN, February 8, 2023

Black boys
need Black men
in their lives.
Doesn't even
need to be their
father. Thank you
to every strong,
admirable Black
man who I had
as a kid.

—Twitter, March 29, 2018

WE DON'T EVEN really talk about the future too much. I put it in the air because I like to talk to the basketball gods out there and see if things can come to fruition. I've always set out goals in my career, talked to the basketball gods, and they've listened to all of them. Hopefully they can listen to this last one, too.

—on playing in the NBA with his oldest son, Bronny,
Sports Illustrated, August 30, 2022

I'VE ALWAYS LOOKED at parenthood, business, and basketball as kind of being the same thing when you are a leader. You have all these different personalities; you have to figure out how to put these personalities in the right place to maximize the team. . . . As a parent, yes, I have three kids and you give them the same structure, but you can't coach them all the same because they are all different people.

—*Kneading Dough: The Podcast*, March 5, 2019

I HAD TO find out how do I tap in to each one of my kids to get the same result but teach them differently. That's the same with being the leader of a basketball team, the leader of a franchise. You can't talk to everyone the same and expect to get the same result or get the most out of them because every personality is different.

—The Tim Ferriss Show, November 27, 2018

I JUST TOLD my wife the other day that I apologize to her. . . . Because the journey that I'm on to want to be the greatest to ever play this game to the point where no one ever forgets what I accomplished, I've at times lost the fact of how important you are to this whole thing. . . . I said I want you to understand that along this journey while I'm playing this game that there will be times where I lose the fact of how important you and my three kids are—my babies are—because of how indebted I am in trying to be cemented in something that will last forever.

—Road Trippin' podcast, March 2017

THE ONLY REASON why I can do what I do at the highest level both on and off the floor is because my best friend got my back regardless the outcome! I'm just the car, she's the engine! Appreciate you Wonder Woman aka Queen

—Instagram, November 14, 2019

SO DAMN PROUD of the Young Man you've become @bronny!! ...Can't believe how fast time is flying by but at the same time I haven't taken 1 second for granted being your dad! Love you kid! Keep leading, being an example to/for your siblings/your peers and most importantly simply just keep being YOU!!!! ThekidfromAKRON 👑 #JamesGang 👑 #BronnyakaHIM 🎥

—Facebook, January 12, 2023

BRONNY, BRYCE, AND Zhuri, my three kids.
They're my treasures, my gems. . . . Bronny,
Bryce, and Z [make] me happy, make me smile
every single day.

—*I Promise Podcast*, October 4, 2022

[THE KIDS] WOULD never understand that
there's a bottom. That's the challenge of a parent
every single day that I have to juggle with: how do
I raise my kids knowing that they'll never feel or
understand what their father went through? But
you give them challenges, and at the end of the
day they are going to walk their own path.

—*Kneading Dough: The Podcast*, March 5, 2019

MAN I'M LITERALLY watching Bronny and Bryce
on the court together for the first time in a game
situation!! This is INSANE!! I'm EMOTIONAL
AF!! WOW

—**Facebook, August 11, 2022**

My family is everything to me. And it's a personal mantra of mine to always be loyal to my family. . . . A family is not a bed of roses, it comes with thorns, and you have to understand that.

—*The Tim Ferriss Show*, November 27, 2018

[MY MOTHER] WAS always a rock. No matter what was going on, she was always a rock and very patient with the process, and I've taken that not only to being a father but in life in general; I always preach this process thing.

—*The Tim Ferriss Show*, November 27, 2018

MY LAST YEAR will be played with my son. Wherever Bronny is at, that's where I'll be. I would do whatever it takes to play with my son for one year. It's not about the money at that point.

—*The Athletic*, February 19, 2022

Part 4

LEGACY

Image

IT'S ALWAYS PRETTY cool to see, the guys that come into our league and they said their favorite player growing up was LeBron James. That means something to me because I feel like I have so much more to do than just playing the game of basketball.

—**postgame press conference, February 20, 2022**

THEN, WHEN MY grandkids show up at some point I'll be able to show them some footage of what their granddad was able to accomplish when he played the game of basketball.

—**postgame press conference, February 20, 2022**

I THINK LEGACY will speak for itself. Who I am as a man and what I do off the floor defines my legacy more than what I do on the court and that's just how I've always thought about it, but I don't really get caught up into it too much.

—***Today Show*, July 6, 2015**

THIS THING IS about more than just basketball.
. . . I can play basketball with my eyes closed
and my hands tied behind my back. The way my
mind, my mind starts working, we could probably
be here for like . . . it could be like midnight.
Someone will have to turn my switch off.

—GQ, February 18, 2014

I'M THE BIGGEST voice that my hometown
has ever seen. . . . I'm the biggest figure that
my hometown has ever seen. I do know that.
I can see that. The responsibility of being the
inspiration and the light for my community—it's
much greater than hitting a jump shot.

—GQ, February 18, 2014

I would hope that people take away that because I was able to play the game at such a high level, that none of that mattered to me because my legacy off the floor was more impactful.

—*I Promise Podcast*, October 4, 2022

I DON'T GIVE a s--- what nobody says. Our quest and our journey is not predicated on what everybody said. You going to have five people that love you out of 10. Then you have five people that hate you out of 10. That's just the way of the land. No matter what you do.

—*Sports Illustrated*, August 30, 2022

A KID WITH a dream from Akron Ohio. Now chopping it up with the Prez [Obama]. Life is Good

—Instagram, January 28, 2013

UP LATE THINKING about life. What's my purpose while I'm here. I'm blessed and will do my very best to continue to inspire the youth!

—Instagram, August 2, 2013

GOOD EVENING LADIES and gentlemen. Captain speaking. My name is LeBron. I would like to welcome you aboard flight 23/6 from Akron to Cleveland to Miami to Cleveland and now in Los Angeles. Thank you for choosing to fly with me. I hope you all enjoy your flight

—**Instagram, September 1, 2019**

I JUST FEEL so good about the game. I feel like I owe it to the game, as long as I could go out and play at a high level, I feel like it's important for me to continue to inspire the youth, continue to inspire my teammates, try to inspire myself, and I still have championship aspiration.

—**ESPN, February 7, 2023**

Love me
or hate me
but at the
end of the
day you will
RESPECT
me!

—Twitter, April 14, 2016

I KNEW WHEN I got drafted as an eighteen-year-old kid that I could play the game of basketball and play it at a high level even against grown men. One thing I didn't know is the success I would have. I prayed on the success, I worked my tail off for the success, but had no idea the success [I would have], and it's just been a very humbling and gratifying, you know, journey, and I hope people have enjoyed it with me.

—**ESPN, February 7, 2023**

HOPEFULLY I MADE an impact enough so people appreciate what I did, and still appreciate what I did off the floor as well, even when I'm done. . . . But I don't live for that. I live for my family, for my friends and my community that needs that voice.

—***New York Times*, February 4, 2023**

Philosophy

I LIKE TO throw things out in the airwaves, but I'm not one to [say] what's going to happen in the next two to three years. I am a visionary, but I'm also a guy that lives in the moment.

—*Sports Illustrated*, August 30, 2022

INSPIRE AND MOTIVATE our youth! Let them know that their dreams can become a reality! That's a responsibility I hold with me every day.

—Twitter, December 15, 2013

I FEEL LIKE I could play for quite a while. So it's all up to my body, but more importantly, my mind. If my mind can stay sharp and fresh and motivated, then the sky's not even a limit for me. I can go beyond that. But we shall see.

—*Sports Illustrated*, August 30, 2022

I don't need motivation from anybody in this league. I motivate myself.

—*New York Times*, June 4, 2021

I DON'T WANT to say it ever becomes too much, but there are times when I wish I could do normal things. . . . I wish I could just walk outside. . . . I wish I could just, like, walk into a movie theater and sit down and go to the concession stand and get popcorn. I wish I could just go to an amusement park just like regular people. I wish I could go to Target sometimes and walk into Starbucks and have my name on the cup just like regular people. . . . I'm not sitting here complaining about it, of course not. But it can be challenging at times.

—*New York Times*, **February 4, 2023**

IT'S MY JOB to make sure that we're as laser-focused as possible, do my job and continue to instill confidence in my teammates until the last horn sounds. . . . That's my job. That's my responsibility. That's my obligation, and I need to continue to do that.

—*New York Times*, **June 5, 2018**

IT'S NOT ABOUT making the shot. . . . It's about having a belief of just taking it, for one, and living with the result.

—*New York Times*, **September 27, 2020**

EVERYONE LIKES TO have their me time. And, of course, I'm one of those guys. But for the most part, with my energy, I don't like being alone. I like being around people and having fun and laughing and being able to give my energy to other people also.

—*Miami Herald*, **February 20, 2011**

I'M VERY MOTIVATED. But I'm right now not in the talking-about-it mode. I've been very quiet this summer for a reason. My mother always told me, "Don't talk about it, be about it." So that's where I'm at.

—**ESPN, September 17, 2020**

No matter
how many
times I fail,
I'll always
be ready
for the next
opportunity.

—Twitter, March 1, 2011

I PUT A lot of pressure on myself not to let my
teammates down. At the end of the day, that's
what it's all about for me. Maybe to a fault at
times, I put so much pressure on myself.

—ESPN, June 15, 2011

I KNOW WHERE I come from, and I know where
my family comes from, and for me to have
milestones along the way—obviously I have more
work to do—but it's cool to see when you're able
to kind of just stop and look at it. Because I don't
get much time to really stop and look at some of
the things that I've done.

—ESPN, November 2, 2015

[READING] JUST SLOWS my mind down. It just
gives me another outlet. Throughout the playoffs
all you think about is basketball. All you want to
do is play basketball. But at the same time it can
become a lot.

—*NBC Sports*, June 21, 2012

NO MATTER IF you come from the top of the top or you come from the bottom of the bottom, you still have a road to travel.

—*Kneading Dough: The Podcast*, **March 5, 2019**

I KNEW THAT money would allow me to access those things, but I never let money get in the way of the drive that I had to get to the top.

—*Kneading Dough: The Podcast*, **March 5, 2019**

I ALWAYS PREACH that the best teacher in life is experience, and it's okay for you to experience defeat. But when you are at a position where you might have to cross that threshold again, do you approach it the same way or do you learn from that?

—*The Tim Ferriss Show*, **November 27, 2018**

WE DON'T NEED more LeBron's, we need more physical therapists, scientists, police officers, teachers, doctors, professors, physicists, computer engineers, etc!! I want every kid to know there is absolutely NO LIMIT to what you can be. Your dreams are there for you to EARN. The teacher/accountant/scientist/dr/etc is just as talented as any athlete, if not more. I can't even begin to tell you guys how many incredible men & women I work with who have never seen the court but are just as vital to our success as I am. There's no way my game is what it is without them. Open your heart & mind to the world around you. See the possible. Dream big. Then work your tail off and chase it.

—Instagram, April 1, 2017

I DON'T LIKE to look at the ending, because I like to just live in the moment.

—*The Tim Ferriss Show*, November 27, 2018

I CAN WATCH *Forensic Files, Martin,* and *The Fresh Prince of Bel-Air* all day long. Sprinkle in a little *Friends*, and I'm good. That's all I need.

—*Road Trippin'* **podcast, February 2018**

I'M A ROUTINE guy. And when my routine is knocked off, it's hard for me to center myself.

—*Road Trippin'* **podcast, December 2020**

PROGRESS OVER PRIDE!! Some of you will never get it but for the ones that will you'll see how much more you can tap into and accomplish!! It's a beautiful thing!

—**Instagram, September 9, 2018**

THE BEST TEACHER in life is experience.

—*SmartLess* **podcast, July 2021**

If life wasn't
a struggle,
there would
be nothing to
accomplish
or overcome.
The struggles
in your life are
positive.

—Twitter, October 25, 2010

I TAKE THAT responsibility and I don't just talk about it, I actually do it as well. So when you come through on your word, it allows the guys that you are leading, male or female, to be able to say, "Okay, we can follow this person because he won't let us down." No matter if it's going good or bad. Every day is not a bed of roses and we understand that, and you have to be able to handle adversity as well.

—*Success! How I Did It*, **May 11, 2017**

FAITH IN YOUR own powers and confidence in your individual methods are essential to success.

—**Twitter, December 29, 2010**

STRUCTURE AND CONSISTENCY creates perfection. You shortcut, you come up short!

—**Twitter, March 6, 2016**

LET'S GO! UP and at it to workouts. 5:38am. No
excuses! #SavageMode #StriveForGreatness

—Twitter, August 18, 2017

I THINK MY career has been like that. It's been
like one of the great rides at Cedar Point in the
sense that you know your stomach drop[s] at
times, you're excited, you're yelling, sometimes
you can't breathe, but you always wanna do it
again.

—ESPN, February 8, 2023

DEFINITELY NOT GOING today without saying
#HappyInternationalWomensDay! Thank
you for being loving, caring, powerful, strong,
ambitious, understanding, dedicated, beautiful,
etc. etc.! This especially to my wife and mother!
Love you all 🖤🖤🖤🖤

—Twitter, March 8, 2018

MY LIFE'S MORE than just basketball... because there's a whole lot more to life! 🙏 ...[I'm] hoping others go out & find their passion & purpose like I've found mine. Because to live a meaningful life requires more!! 👑 💧

—**Facebook, February 16, 2023**

WHEN YOU PUT in the work, the results will happen.... If you didn't put in the work, that's when you get worried.

—*New York Times*, **August 21, 2020**

The GOAT

Debate

My MOTIVATION IS this ghost I'm chasing. The ghost played in Chicago.

—*Sports Illustrated*, August 2, 2016

My CAREER IS totally different than Michael Jordan's. What I've gone through is totally different than what he went through. What he did was unbelievable, and I watched it unfold. I looked up to him so much. I think it's cool to put myself in position to be one of those great players, but if I can ever put myself in position to be the greatest player, that would be something extraordinary.

—*Sports Illustrated*, August 2, 2016

I'VE ALWAYS PRIDED myself on saying, "I wanna be the greatest to ever play this game." And that came from a motivation to myself, my drive to be the greatest of all time.

—ABC News, February 8, 2023

I want to be, if not the greatest, one of the greatest to ever play this game, and I will continue to work for that and continue to put on this uniform and be the best I can be every night.

—postgame press conference, June 21, 2013

I always feel like I'm the best to ever play this game, but you know there's so many other great ones and I'm happy to just be a part of their journey.

—*House of Highlights*, February 8, 2023

MY DRIVE TO be the greatest basketball player
ever is very high.

—*GQ*, February 18th, 2014

GOT LIKE 50 pictures of MJ on my wall—that's
all you need to know about me. Got Iverson,
McGrady, Magic, and Kobe on there, too. And
myself. I'm on my wall.

—ESPN, December 23, 2002

I'M NOT MJ, I'm LJ.

—Twitter, February 13, 2013

IT'S NO COMPARISON to him. I think people
always try to figure out ways or want to compare
someone to someone. But you know, Mike is
Mike and I'm LeBron and I'm trying to make my
own name, make my own statement.

—*South Florida Sun-Sentinel*, February 15, 2013

YOU CAN DEBATE who's the greatest of all time
individually, things of that nature, and what
they've done. But as far as the teams that's won
two of the hardest championship in Lakers
history, I've been a part of that.

—*Road Trippin'* **podcast, December 2020**

BEING IN THE conversation so much about
being a part of the all-time greats, it's always
humbling to me. I really don't get caught up in the
comparison.

—*Road Trippin'* **podcast, June 2017**

Milestones

1984

- LeBron Raymone James (Sr.) is born on December 30, 1984, in Akron, Ohio, to Gloria Marie James and Anthony McClelland. His father is absent from his life, so he is raised by his 16-year-old single mother. They often move from one neighborhood to another as his mother seeks work.

1988

- James receives a miniature basketball hoop and ball on Christmas Day, thus introducing him to the game that will immortalize him in NBA history.

1993

- After being spotted playing football with some other kids, eight-year-old James is invited to play youth football by coach Bruce Kelker. James's mother says she can't pay for James's equipment or transport him to practice, but Kelker tells her he'll take care of everything, determined to get James on his new team. Kelker fosters James's talent, outfits him with everything he needs to play, and takes him to and from practice. However, when going to pick up James, he often discovers that James and his mother have once again moved. In response, Kelker invites James and his mother to live with him so his star player can attend games.

- Frank Walker, another local youth football coach, sees that space is growing tight in Kelker's household and, wanting to keep James in Akron with his mother and playing football, houses James with his wife and three children, giving James his first taste of a stable home life. Here, James is formally introduced to the game of basketball by Walker and allowed to practice once he finishes all of his homework.

1997

- James wins his first MVP title for helping lead his team, the Shooting Stars, to victory in the 12-and-younger division of the Youth Basketball of America national tournament.

1999

- James chooses to attend St. Vincent–St. Mary High School, a private Catholic school with a predominantly white student body, with his "Fab Four" friends he met while playing in the Amateur Athletic Union.

- As a freshman, James plays for the Fighting Irish on St. Vincent–St. Mary's varsity basketball team.

2000

- James helps lead the St. Vincent–St. Mary varsity basketball team to their first of three state titles and an undefeated 27–0 season.

2001

- James becomes the first high school sophomore to be named Ohio's Mr. Basketball.

- James leads the Fighting Irish varsity basketball team to their second consecutive state championship.

- He becomes the first high school sophomore to be selected for the *USA Today* All-USA First Team.

- James is featured in a *Slam* magazine article and touted as someone who "might just be the best high school basketball player in America right now."

2002

- At just 17 years old, James appears on the cover of *Sports Illustrated* with the headline "The Chosen One."

- James is consecutively named Ohio's Mr. Basketball and selected for the *USA Today* All-USA First Team. He is also named the *USA Today* Player of the Year for boys' high school basketball.

- During his senior year, James makes his debut on national television playing against the top-ranked school in the country, Oak Hill Academy. The game is broadcast on ESPN2 and James's team wins 65–45, with James scoring 31 points.

2003

- James becomes the first person to win the title of Ohio's Mr. Basketball three years in a row.

- James finishes his high school basketball career with the Fighting Irish's third state title in the four years he plays on the team.

- James is selected for the *USA Today* All-USA First Team for the third year in a row, and is named the *USA Today* High School Player of the Year for the second year in a row.

- James is chosen as the first overall pick in the 2003 NBA draft for his hometown team, the Cleveland Cavaliers.

- He plays his first professional basketball game as a Cavalier on October 29 against the Sacramento Kings. Sadly, the team loses 106–92, despite an impressive debut performance from James.

2004

- James becomes the first Cavalier and the youngest player ever to be named the NBA Rookie of the Year.

- James founds the LeBron James Family Foundation in his hometown of Akron, Ohio.

- James debuts on the U.S. Men's National Basketball Team at the Summer Olympics in Athens, Greece. However, Team USA finishes with a bronze medal—breaking a streak of winning gold in the Olympics since 1992.

- James's first child, LeBron Raymone "Bronny" James Jr., is born on October 6.

2005

- James plays in his first NBA All-Star Game, becoming the second-youngest player to participate in an All-Star Game.

2006

- James is once again selected to play in the NBA All-Star Game and earns his first All-Star MVP award.

2007

- After winning their first-ever Eastern Conference championship in franchise history, the Cavaliers and James both make their first NBA Finals appearance. They are defeated by the San Antonio Spurs in a four-game sweep.

- James's second son, Bryce, is born on June 14 amid the 2007 NBA Finals against the San Antonio Spurs.

- In one of his first forays into television, James hosts the 33rd series premiere of *Saturday Night Live*, with Kanye West featured as the musical guest.

2008

- James becomes the youngest player in NBA history to score 10,000 career points at 23 years and 59 days.

- James becomes the 2007–2008 NBA scoring champion after averaging 30 points per game that season.

- James joins the 2008 Olympic national team, nicknamed the "Redeem Team" after their poor performance during the 2004 Olympics. Team USA is undefeated and wins the gold medal in Beijing, the team's first gold since 2000.

2009

- James wins his first NBA MVP award for helping lead the Cavaliers to their franchise-best record of 66–16.

- James and the Cavaliers once again make it to the NBA Eastern Conference Finals. Though they are favored to win and make it to the NBA Finals, the Cavaliers lose to the Orlando Magic.

2010

- James wins his second consecutive NBA MVP award, becoming only the 10th player in NBA history to win back-to-back MVP awards.

- On July 8, James's controversial decision to leave the Cleveland Cavaliers—who hadn't won a championship during James's time on the team—for the Miami Heat is televised on ESPN in a special called *The Decision*. In the time after *The Decision* airs, James draws heavy criticism from fans and professionals in the industry alike. Fans take to burning his Cavaliers jersey and legendary players like Michael Jordan and Magic Johnson critique James for the move to Miami. Although *The Decision* raises over $3 million for charity, the backlash against James overshadows the ESPN special's philanthropic impact.

- Cleveland Cavaliers owner Dan Gilbert pens an open letter to Cavalier fans denouncing James, calling his actions "heartless and callous" and a "cowardly betrayal" of the team and its fans.

- James is featured in the "People Who Mattered" section of *Time*'s Person of the Year issue, both for his consecutive MVP awards and impressive performance with the Cavaliers earlier that year and for his horrible ending with the Cavaliers before his contentious departure from the team for the Miami Heat.

2011

- James makes it to the NBA Finals with the Miami Heat. Despite forming a "Big 3" with fellow Heat players Dwyane Wade and Chris Bosh and being a favorite to win the Finals, James gives one of his lowest-scoring Finals performances, and the Heat loses in Game 6 to the Dallas Mavericks.

- The LeBron James Family Foundation launches the I PROMISE program, which today serves over 1,400 students across several Akron public schools by providing programs, resources, and mentorship to help them succeed in the classroom.

- Through the LeBron James Family Foundation, the new Wheels for Education program begins. With the support of various sponsors, laptops, school supplies, and bicycles are provided for each student in the program to help them stay in school and succeed all the way to graduation.

- James is inducted into St. Vincent–St. Mary's athletic hall of fame with several of his Fighting Irish teammates and friends.

2012

- James wins his first NBA championship with the Miami Heat and his first championship overall in his professional career, and earns both the regular-season and Finals MVP awards.

- James once again plays for Team USA in the London Olympics and helps lead the team to their second straight gold medal. He joins NBA legend Michael Jordan as the only two players to win an NBA MVP award, an NBA championship, the NBA Finals MVP, and an Olympic gold medal all in the same year.

- James is named the *Sports Illustrated* Sportsman of the Year.

- James is chosen as the Male Athlete of the Year by USA Basketball for helping win the gold medal at the Olympics and leading the Miami Heat to win the NBA championship.

2013

- James becomes the youngest player in NBA history to score 20,000 points and surpass the 5,000-assist threshold.

- James marries his high school sweetheart Savannah James née Brinson on September 14.

- James wins his second NBA championship with the Heat, and his second championship overall, against the San Antonio Spurs. He once again earns MVP awards for both the Finals and the regular season, and becomes the youngest to win four regular-season MVP awards.

- The LeBron James Arena at St. Vincent–St. Mary High School, newly renovated due to a $1 million donation from James, opens.

2014

- The Miami Heat becomes the first team to win four consecutive Eastern Conference championships since the Boston Celtics during the 1984–1987 NBA seasons.

- James scores his career-best of 61 points in a single game against the Charlotte Bobcats, who become the Charlotte Hornets in the following season.

- After defeating the San Antonio Spurs the year previous, James plays against the Spurs once again in the Finals on the Heat's quest for a Finals championship three-peat. Unfortunately, the Heat loses by a 4–1 margin.

- After his 2013–2014 season with the Heat, James becomes a free agent once again.

- In an essay published in *Sports Illustrated*, four years after announcing his move to the Miami Heat, James announces his return home, re-signing with the Cleveland Cavaliers in hopes of fulfilling his mission of bringing a championship to his hometown. James writes, "what's most important for me is bringing one trophy back to Northeast Ohio. I always believed that I'd return to Cleveland and finish my career there." He closes his essay by telling Akron, Ohio, and Cavaliers fans, "I'm coming home." Compared to *The Decision*, his essay and announcement of returning to Cleveland are well-received by fans and met with excitement.

- James's only daughter, Zhuri, is born on October 22.

2015

- In a partnership between the LeBron James Family Foundation and the University of Akron, eligible I PROMISE students are guaranteed a fully funded, four-year scholarship to the university to further pursue their education.

- James becomes the youngest player to score 25,000 career points at 30 years and 307 days, beating Kobe Bryant's previous record by over a year.

- James helps lead the Cavaliers to the NBA Finals against the Golden State Warriors. However, after losing Kevin Love and Kyrie Irving to injuries, the Cavaliers are bested 2–4. James is lauded for his performance during the Finals and for becoming the first player in NBA Finals history to lead both Finals teams in points, assists, and rebounds for the entire series.

2016

- The Cavaliers fire head coach David Blatt, with many noting the obvious tension between Blatt and James since the 2015 Finals. The Cavaliers' assistant coach Tyronn Lue steps in as the new head coach.

- James finally fulfills his promise to Cleveland and leads the Cleveland Cavaliers to win their first-ever NBA championship—and the city's first championship title in more than 50 years—beating the Golden State Warriors after coming back from a 3–1 deficit. The Cavaliers become the first team in NBA Finals history to recover from a 3–1 deficit and win. After their win, James emotionally tells Cavaliers fans, "Cleveland, this is for you." His stunning performance unanimously secures his third Finals MVP award.

- The LeBron James Family Foundation establishes the I PROMISE Institute at the University of Akron as a resource center to help I PROMISE students thrive in college.

- James receives his second Sportsperson of the Year honor from *Sports Illustrated*.

2017

- James receives the J. Walter Kennedy Citizenship Award from the Professional Basketball Writers Association for the 2016–2017 season in recognition of his philanthropic work and service to the Akron community, and for his commitment to improving educational opportunities for the youth of Akron through the LeBron James Family Foundation.

- James also receives the NAACP Jackie Robinson Sports Award, becoming the first athlete in nearly two decades to receive the award after it was retired in 1999. This award is bestowed upon James for his "high achievement in athletics and [his] contributions in the pursuit of social justice, civil rights, and community involvement."

- The Cavaliers make it to the NBA Finals for their third straight season to face off against the Golden State Warriors for the third consecutive year. James becomes the first player in NBA history to record a triple-double average in the Finals, but the Cavaliers ultimately lose to the Warriors.

2018

- James sets an NBA record of scoring double digits in 867 consecutive games.

- The Cavaliers make it to their fourth Finals in a row—and James's eighth consecutive championship appearance—once again facing the Golden State Warriors, but are defeated in overtime for Game 1. As a result of the loss, James punches his hand into a whiteboard in the locker room, sustaining a severe bone contusion. He continues to play in the next three games of the Finals, but his injury affects his performance. The Cavaliers are swept in four games, the first Finals sweep since 2007 when the LeBron-led Cavaliers were swept by the San Antonio Spurs.

- In July, James officially signs with the Los Angeles Lakers. The announcement is met with a more positive reaction compared to his previous move to the Miami Heat.

- The LeBron James Family Foundation's I PROMISE School, a public elementary school devoted to helping struggling students stay in school, officially opens in James's hometown of Akron, Ohio, welcoming 240 students on the first day of school.

- *The Shop: Uninterrupted,* a talk show starring James and his lifelong friend and business partner Maverick Carter, premieres on HBO. The show features celebrity guests as they have honest conversations and discussions with James and Carter inside a U.S. barbershop.

- On Christmas Day, James and the Lakers face the Golden State Warriors and win by a large margin. However, James sustains a groin injury, the first major injury of his career, causing him to miss 17 consecutive games.

2019

- As a result of James's groin injury, James is eventually ruled out for the remainder of the 2018–2019 season, only playing a total of 55 games for the season. The Lakers end up failing to make it to the playoffs for the sixth season in a row, marking the first time James is absent from the playoffs since the 2004–2005 season. This also breaks James's eight-year streak of appearing in every NBA Finals since 2011.

- James is named by *Time* as one of the 100 most influential people in the world for the fourth time, after previously making the list in 2005, 2013, and 2017.

- The LeBron James Family Foundation announces the I PROMISE Village, which provides I PROMISE students and their families a safe place to stay if they are experiencing homelessness, domestic violence, and other extreme circumstances.

2020

- Kent State University joins the University of Akron in offering I PROMISE students free tuition to pursue their degrees.

- With the help of the LeBron James Family Foundation, James hosts a virtual graduation for the Class of 2020, as graduation ceremonies are canceled and moved online due to the ongoing COVID-19 pandemic. The graduation is broadcast on major TV networks and streamed on various social media platforms, with appearances from celebrity guests such as Barack Obama, Megan Rapinoe, and Zendaya to celebrate the graduating class and honor their achievements amid an unconventional year.

- James cofounds SpringHill Company, an entertainment development and production company, with his business partner Maverick Carter. Named for the apartment complex in Akron, Ohio, where James moved in sixth grade, the company unites three earlier companies James and Carter had founded together and seeks to empower and elevate diverse creators and their communities.

- Despite playing in an abbreviated season due to the COVID-19 pandemic, James leads the Lakers to their first Pacific Division title since 2012, their first top seed in the Western Conference playoffs since the 2009–2010 season, and ultimately victory in the NBA Finals against his former team, the Miami Heat. He secures his fourth championship and fourth Finals MVP award, becoming the second-oldest player in the league's history to win the award and the only player in the NBA's history to win the award in three different franchises.

- James becomes the first athlete to be named the *Sports Illustrated* Sportsperson of the Year three times, having previously won the award in 2012 and 2016.

- James receives the 2020 *Sports Illustrated* Muhammad Ali Legacy Award for his social activism in the midst of COVID-19, police brutality, and voter suppression. Ali's widow, Lonnie Ali, says James "continues to embody Muhammad's principles and core beliefs, using his celebrity platform to champion social justice and political causes that uplift all people."

- James is named *Time*'s Athlete of the Year for founding the nonprofit More Than a Vote in response to the racial injustice and police brutality that mark much of the year to spur voters, especially Black voters, to vote in the 2020 presidential election despite historic voter suppression efforts. James recruits prominent athletes from all over the sports world to take part in the organization, vote, and urge fans to follow in their footsteps. More Than a Vote also seeks to open sports arenas as polling places on Election Day and to enlist younger people to replace older poll workers due to health concerns from the COVID-19 pandemic. He is heralded for being one of the first prominent sports figures to bridge the gap between commercial appeal and political duty, something many athletes had been reticent to do for fear of tarnishing their image.

- On his 36th birthday, James becomes the first player in NBA history to score double-digit points in 1,000 consecutive games.

2021

- James sustains a high ankle sprain during a game against the Atlanta Hawks. The Lakers announce that James will be out indefinitely for the rest of the season. In total, James misses 26 games—the highest number of absences in a season throughout his career. James and the Lakers later make it to the NBA play-offs, but due to numerous player injuries and James still recovering from his own injury, the Lakers lose against the Phoenix Suns. This marks the first time James has lost in the first round of the playoffs.

- James receives the President's Award at the 52nd annual NAACP Image Awards for his "leadership, sportsmanship, and commitment to social justice," recognizing "his work both on and off the court," including the work he has done through the LeBron James Family Foundation and More Than a Vote.

- James stars in *Space Jam: A New Legacy*, a sequel/reboot of the original *Space Jam* that starred NBA legend Michael Jordan.

- James is selected to the NBA 75th Anniversary Team, an honor that names the greatest players in league history. James is one of 11 players chosen who are still active in the 2021–2022 season and one of four players playing for the Los Angeles Lakers.

2022

- James becomes the only player in NBA history to record at least 10,000 points, 10,000 rebounds, and 10,000 assists.

- In April, the Lakers announce that due to a left ankle injury sustained during a game against the New Orleans Pelicans, James will sit out for the remainder of the 2021–2022 season in order to recover.

- *Forbes* declares James to be a billionaire. He is the first NBA player to become a billionaire while still actively playing.

- James re-signs with the Lakers on a two-year, $97.1 million contract, making him the highest-paid athlete in NBA history.

- James is featured alongside his sons on the cover of *Sports Illustrated*, entitled "The Chosen Sons," an echo of James's first appearance on the magazine cover titled "The Chosen One" 20 years earlier.

- James voices his desire to play professional basketball beside his sons Bronny, who will be eligible for the draft in 2024, and Bryce, who will be eligible in 2027.

2023

- James is selected to play at the 2023 NBA All-Star Game, tying with former Laker Kareem Abdul-Jabbar for the most All-Star selections at 19. The 2023 game marks James's 19th consecutive All-Star appearance, and also sets a record for most All-Star games played, breaking Kareem Abdul-Jabbar's former record of 18.

- On January 31, James breaks into the top five and moves up to fourth place on the NBA career assists list with a total of 10,338 assists.

- On February 7, James becomes the leading scorer in all of the NBA, surpassing former Laker Kareem Abdul-Jabbar's nearly 39-year-old record and scoring his 38,388th career point.

- The Lakers defeat the Golden State Warriors, the defending 2022 NBA champions, to secure their place in the 2023 Western Conference Finals. James wins his 41st playoff series, the most in NBA history.

- James and the Lakers make it to the Conference Finals but are swept by the Denver Nuggets in four games. This is the first time James loses in the Conference Finals since 2009 with the Cavaliers against the Orlando Magic.

Acknowledgments

We would like to thank Henry Begler, Johnna Caboz, Kelsey Dame, Madelyn Erickson, Paige Gilberg, Mira Green, Eva Lopez, Julia Poetzinger, Emma Ramirez, Erin Rosenberg, Madiha Saber, Suzanne Sonnier, and Connor White for their invaluable contributions to the preparation of this manuscript.